SANKOFA
BLACK HERITAGE COLLECTION

MUSIC

NADIA L. HOHN

SERIES EDITOR • TOM HENDERSON

www.rubiconpublishing.com

Associate Publisher: Amy Land
Project Editor: Jessica Rose
Editorial Assistant: Sarah Adams
Creative Director: Jennifer Drew
Lead Designer: Sherwin Flores
Graphic Designers: Jen Harvey, Stacy Jarvis, Robin Lindner, Jason Mitchell

Every reasonable effort has been made to trace the owners of copyrighted
material and to make due acknowledgement. Any errors or omissions
drawn to our attention will be gladly rectified in future editions.

15 16 17 18 19   5 4 3 2 1

ISBN: 978-1-77058-945-2

Printed in China

CONTENTS

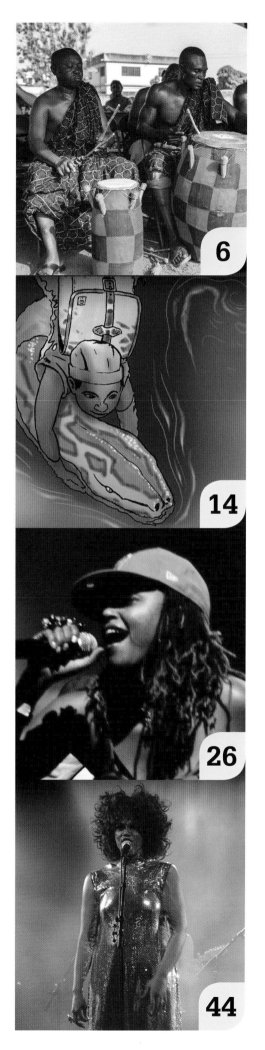

Music

Music is used by cultures around the world as a form of expression. History, traditions, and experiences can all be represented in different styles of music. When we hear a piece of music, we are able to recognize the feelings of a musician, and maybe even relate to these feelings ourselves.

Music does not only bring people together. It can also be a part of an amazing career or even a tool for change.

Why is music an important part of the human experience?

INSTRUMENTS

WHEN YOU THINK about traditional African music, what do you think about? It's possible that you might think about drumming. But did you know there are many different kinds of African drums and other traditional instruments? Read these short reports to learn more.

DJEMBE

The djembe originated in Mali. To make a djembe, an animal skin is tied to a hardwood shell. The djembe is a common instrument found at drum circles all over the world. Drum circles are a way to bring people together through music.

TALKING DRUM

Many researchers think that talking drums came from the Yoruba and Hausa people of West Africa. However, the drum's many names show that it was used in other parts of Africa, too. To play a talking drum, you strike it with a stick and squeeze its middle. The sounds it makes sound similar to a human voice.

During the transatlantic slave trade, millions of Africans were brought to North, Central, and South America. In many places, enslaved Africans were not allowed to make or play musical instruments. Some owners of enslaved Africans worried that music would be used to communicate escape plans.

KORA

The kora is a stringed instrument that is played by plucking the strings. Enslaved Africans in the United States used the same construction methods to create a very similar instrument, which eventually became the banjo.

OF AFRICA

MBIRA

The *mbira* is also known as a thumb piano. However, instead of pressing down on keys to play a mbira, you pluck pieces of metal. The mbira originated in southern and eastern Africa.

KPANLOGO

Ghanaian drums range in size, sound, and function. One type of Ghanaian drum is the *kpanlogo*. The Ewe people of eastern Ghana are known around the world for their complex rhythms. In different Ewe music genres, such as Habobo and Agbadza, drummers play different rhythms for different purposes and ceremonies.

Ghanaian musicians playing drums

BRAZILIAN SAMBA DRUMS

The *surdo*, *Qweeka*, *repinique*, *pandeiro*, *tamborim*, and *caixa* are all drums used in Brazilian samba. Samba is an Afro-Brazilian drumming tradition that dates back to the 17th century. There are different forms of samba. *Samba de roda* is the original form and was practised in Bahia, a state in Brazil. Performers participated in ceremonies for Candomblé, a traditional religion. When the ceremony was complete, participants would have fun by getting into the "roda," or circle, to continue to drum, sing, and dance.

Brazilian men drum in Bahia.

BODY PERCUSSION

In the United States, enslaved Africans were forbidden to play drums. However, this did not stop them from creating rhythms and songs. Juba dance (sometimes called hambone) is a style of African music that was developed to use the whole body. Juba involves using hands to slap parts of the body, such as the thighs, shins, cheeks, and hands, to create sounds. Other types of body percussion that came out of Juba are step dance and beat box. Like tap dancing, step dance uses a dancer's feet to create rhythm. Beat box uses the voice to create sounds similar to drums.

Step Afrika! performs.

ALFAIA DRUM

The *alfaia* drum is one type of drum used in *maracatu*, a traditional Afro-Brazilian performance style. Maracatu features musical instruments, costumes, dancers, songs, and characters. It originated during the time of slavery, when enslaved Africans in Brazil were assigned leadership roles like the king and queen. Even though slavery ended in Brazil in 1888, maracatu processions continue. Today, there are maracatu groups all over Brazil and around the world.

ATABAQUE DRUM

The *atabaque* drum is one of a few instruments used in capoeira, a martial art that originated in Brazil as early as the 16th century. Capoeira combines quick and acrobatic movements, dance, indigenous Brazilian fight styles, and musical instruments. Enslaved Africans used capoeira as a means of protecting their *quilombos*. Quilombos were rural communities where many escaped enslaved Africans lived. Today, people practise capoeira for fun, fitness, and self-defence.

AFRO-CUBAN DRUMS

Afro-Cuban culture has given the world several musical genres and types of musical instruments. Popular styles like rumba and salsa originated in Cuba, and have also influenced other types of music, including African genres like Ghanaian highlife and Afrobeat. One thing that makes Afro-Cuban music unique is the use of its drums, which are constructed in similar ways to ancient African drums.

CAJÓN

You can hear the cajón, also called a rumba box, in Afro-Cuban music as well as Jamaican mento. However, this instrument came all the way from Peru and was constructed by enslaved Africans. The enslaved Africans took shipping crates and planks to construct cajóns, which are similar to an instrument played in Angola. The cajón is played by sitting on it and striking the wooden surface.

mento: *style of folk music*

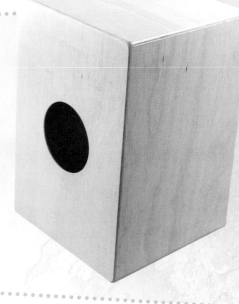

STEEL DRUMS

Steel drums were created through recycling and resistance. When African drums were banned in Trinidad, people found other objects, such as frying pans and oil drums, to create rhythms to play at carnival time. Carnival is an annual event with colourful costumes, music, and many other traditions. Today, steel drums are played throughout the world.

Steel drummers from the CIS Band Trust play steel drums at the Notting Hill Panorama Championships in Hyde Park, London, England.

CONNECT IT

Festivals across Canada celebrate traditional African music. Go online and choose one of these festivals. Create a poster that advertises this festival, making sure to include the most important information about it.

REVOLUTION FROM DE BEAT

◼ BY LILLIAN ALLEN

THINK ABOUT IT

Revolution is the overthrow of a government or system. With a partner, discuss how music might play a role in revolution.

"Riddim" is the Jamaican patois pronunciation of the word "rhythm." Try reading this poem out loud. Can you hear the rhythm in the words?

ABOUT THE POET

Jamaican-born poet, professor, writer, activist, and musician Lillian Allen lives in Toronto, Ontario. She is one of the originators of dub poetry. Dub poetry is a type of rhythmic performance poetry that is often about political issues. Allen has received several awards for her work. These awards include two Juno awards and a Canadian Congress of Black Women award for contributions to "Black culture in particular and Canadian culture in general."

Revolution from de drum
Revolution from de beat
Revolution from de heart
Revolution with de feet

➤ De riddim and the heave and the sway of the beat
de rumblings and the tumblings down
to the dreams to the beat. To the impulse to be free
to the life that spring up in the heat   in the heat
in the pounding dance to be free
to bust open a window
crash upon a door
strip the crust of confinement
seep truth, through cracks
through the routing rhythms of the musical tracts   tracks

De sound of reggae music came on a wave of patter   patter
of deeply rooted internal chatter   chatter
on wings of riddim and melodies gone free
the bass strum the heart
the bass drum the heart beat
and the Rastaman pound! Bong bong   bong bong
beat them drums mon! Bong bong   bong bong

And de sound all around
and the voice
of impulse crafted into life burning darkness
of light
of days journeying through the night
of riddim pulse wails and dreams
and determination to be free
of sight
of a vision that ignites

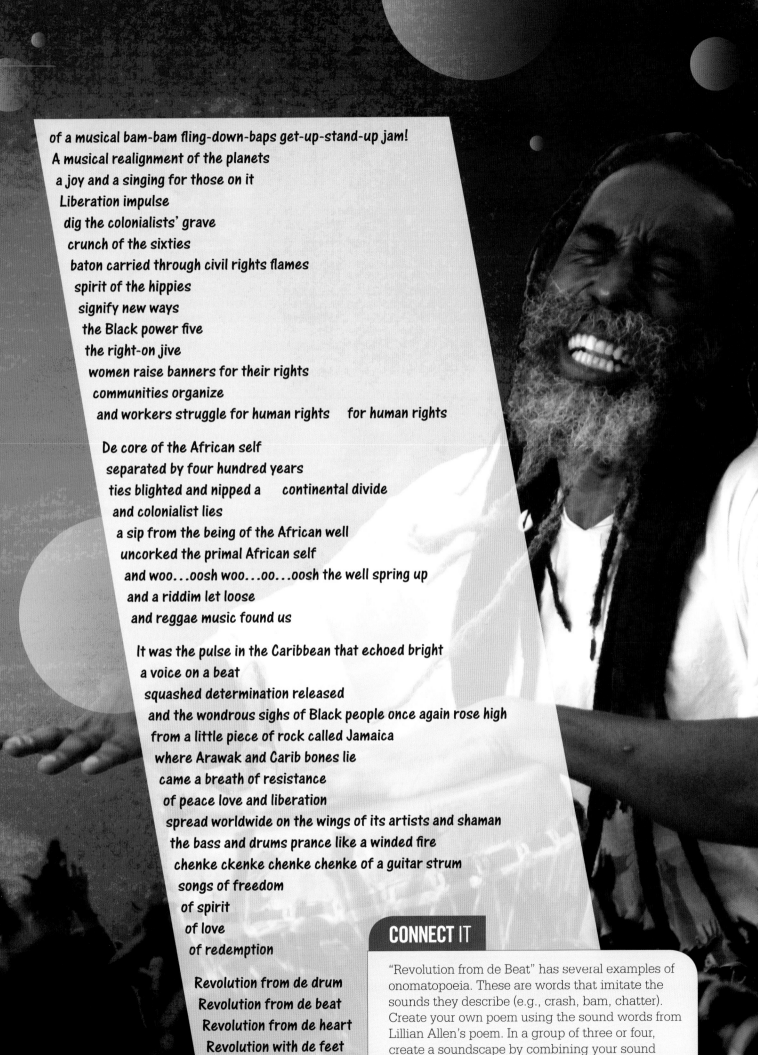

of a musical bam-bam fling-down-baps get-up-stand-up jam!
A musical realignment of the planets
a joy and a singing for those on it
Liberation impulse
dig the colonialists' grave
crunch of the sixties
baton carried through civil rights flames
spirit of the hippies
signify new ways
the Black power five
the right-on jive
women raise banners for their rights
communities organize
and workers struggle for human rights   for human rights

De core of the African self
separated by four hundred years
ties blighted and nipped a   continental divide
and colonialist lies
a sip from the being of the African well
uncorked the primal African self
and woo...oosh woo...oo...oosh the well spring up
and a riddim let loose
and reggae music found us

It was the pulse in the Caribbean that echoed bright
a voice on a beat
squashed determination released
and the wondrous sighs of Black people once again rose high
from a little piece of rock called Jamaica
where Arawak and Carib bones lie
came a breath of resistance
of peace love and liberation
spread worldwide on the wings of its artists and shaman
the bass and drums prance like a winded fire
chenke ckenke chenke chenke of a guitar strum
songs of freedom
of spirit
of love
of redemption

Revolution from de drum
Revolution from de beat
Revolution from de heart
Revolution with de feet
Ah revolution

CONNECT IT

"Revolution from de Beat" has several examples of onomatopoeia. These are words that imitate the sounds they describe (e.g., crash, bam, chatter). Create your own poem using the sound words from Lillian Allen's poem. In a group of three or four, create a soundscape by combining your sound poems into a performance. A soundscape is a sound or combination of sounds used to tell a story.

11

10 THINGS
YOU MAYBE DIDN'T KNOW ABOUT
K'NAAN

THINK ABOUT IT

K'Naan and his family were forced to flee their homeland because of war. What things, people, or culture do you think K'Naan would have had trouble leaving behind? Explain your answer to a partner.

K'NAAN IS A Somali-born Canadian rapper. He is also a storyteller with a passion for bringing people together through art. He uses his own experiences to connect with others and to bring awareness to global issues. Read this list to learn more about K'Naan and his work.

Somalia

QUICK FACTS

Name: Keinan Warsame (a.k.a. K'Naan)
Born: 30 May 1978, in Mogadishu, Somalia
Occupations: rapper, singer, poet, instrumentalist

1 His love of hip hop helped him learn English.

Growing up in Somalia, K'Naan received hip-hop records in the mail from his father, who had immigrated to the United States. By listening to these records, K'Naan learned the basics of the English language by copying the lyrics phonetically. After a while, K'Naan was writing poetry in English and posting it on Somali websites.

2 He has a talented family.

K'Naan's aunt Magool was one of Africa's best-known singers. Her nickname translates as "the mother of the Somali art of singers." K'Naan's grandfather Haji Mohamed was a gifted poet.

phonetically: *by writing words in the way that they sound (instead of how they are actually spelled)*

3 He performed for the United Nations.

K'Naan performed for the United Nations High Commissioner for Refugees in 1999. K'Naan's spoken word piece criticized the UN for its unsuccessful aid missions to Somalia in the 1990s.

4 His famous anthem "Wavin' Flag" brings people together in celebration and aid.

The song from K'Naan's album *Troubadour* was used in the 2010 FIFA World Cup. The song was then re-recorded in Vancouver during the Olympic Games to benefit the 2010 earthquake in Haiti. "Wavin' Flag" would eventually raise over $1 million for disaster relief in Haiti.

5 Canada has recognized his talents.

K'Naan is the winner of multiple Juno awards. His first album, *Dusty Foot Philosopher*, won Rap Recording of the Year in 2006. His second album, *Troubadour*, won two Juno awards for Artist of the Year and Songwriter of the Year in 2010. His 2012 album, *Country, God or the Girl*, had its first single reach number 14 on the Billboard Canadian Hot 100.

6 His songs have been featured onscreen.

K'Naan's music was featured in the 2010 film *The Karate Kid*. His music has also appeared on TV shows, such as *Grey's Anatomy* and *Jimmy Kimmel Live*.

7 He is an activist.

In 2011, K'Naan, along with U2 singer Bono, worked to raise awareness about the drought in Somalia and East Africa. In speaking to reporters about the cause, K'Naan said, "We are seeing a new generation of young leaders who will not take the victim's seat, but who instead stand proudly with an activated devotion."

8 His writing extends beyond music.

K'Naan has written articles for magazines and newspapers, including *NOW Magazine* and the *New York Times*. He has written articles about many topics, including his music, his life in Somalia, and Black History Month.

9 He is a children's book author.

In 2012, K'Naan published a children's book called *When I Get Older: The Story Behind "Wavin' Flag."* The book tells the story of K'Naan's experiences growing up in Somalia and coming to Canada as a teenager. K'Naan's grandfather and his poetry were a part of the inspiration for "Wavin' Flag," the song that inspired the book.

10 He is a screenwriter and aspiring filmmaker.

In 2013, K'Naan's first script, *Maanokoobiyo*, was chosen as one of 13 projects for the annual Sundance Institute's Directors and Screenwriters Labs. His script is about an artistic orphan named Maano who joins a mercenary squad. K'Naan hopes to film his movie in Somalia. He will use many of his own childhood experiences as inspiration for the film.

Refugees: *people who are forced to leave their country for safety reasons*
drought: *long period of dry weather*
screenwriter: *person who writes film scripts*
aspiring: *working toward something*
mercenary: *hired soldier*

CONNECT IT

K'Naan's "Wavin' Flag" has been recorded in many languages. Use the Internet to find the different versions of the song and watch the videos. Choose your favourite version, and write a short paragraph explaining why you chose it.

THE LOST TOUMKAK

BY NJACKO BACKO

IN WEST AFRICA, the history of a people is passed down through the oral tradition by a griot (also called a jeli). Griots are storytellers. Some griots use poetry, others sing or play music, and many do all three. Some stories describe historical events and others feature a moral. This traditional story comes to us from Cameroon-born musician and storyteller Njacko Backo.

ABOUT THE AUTHOR

Njacko Backo is a storyteller, author, educator, musician, and dancer. He was born in Cameroon, and now lives in Toronto, Ontario.

Deep in the heart of Africa, in the hills of Cameroon, lies a beautiful little village called Bazoula. Many years ago, thieves came to Bazoula and stole the spiritual drum of the tribe called the Toumkak. Ever since that time, the harvests had been consistently scarce. Everyone in the village knew that it was the gods of the ancestors who caused the droughts because they were upset that they no longer heard the sound of the Toumkak. Many brave villagers had left to retrieve the Toumkak, never to return.

One morning in Bazoula, a little boy named Ngata was born. His parents loved each other deeply, and joyfully welcomed their new son. Years passed, and the family thrived. When the little boy came to be nine years old, his Dad fell in love with another beautiful maiden in the village. They got married, and soon after that, the Dad's second wife got pregnant and gave birth to twins. The whole family celebrated the birth.

A few weeks later, the Dad started to change. All of his attention went to the twins and his new wife. He no longer loved Ngata's Mother. There was a lot of fighting and unhappiness, and Ngata's Mother became ill and died.

Shortly thereafter, Ngata's Dad called his son and said, "My little boy, you are brave. You know that the village Toumkak was stolen by the mean people of Nyakabouga. I want you to go there and to bring me back that drum so that I will be the King of Bazoula!"

Stunned, Ngata left and ran to tell his Grandmother. The Grandmother started to cry. "Oh! Your Mother passed away because of your Father's hatred. Now, he wants to put his poisonous hatred on you!"

She prayed to the ancestors for guidance and said, "My little boy, tonight you will sleep here." Happiness came to Ngata's heart because he loved being with his Grandmother. That night, Ngata's Grandmother didn't sleep at all. She ground some dry corn, mixed it with organic honey, and baked it into a delicious cake. She put it in a bag along with a calabash full of water.

Early in the morning, Ngata was up and eager to help his Grandmother on the farm. His Grandmother said, "No, today you will start your journey. Take this bag and listen to me closely. Whenever you have a problem on your journey, you need to sing this song:

Yê beu neutoueu neutoueu
Toumkak beu bieun veulah ben noh
Toumkak, toumkak, ou ba ya di ôh
Toumkak, toumkak, ou ba ya di yê

"Go! The gods of our ancestors are with you." His Grandmother kissed him, blessed him, and sent him on his way.

After two days of travelling in the forest, Ngata found himself at a lake. But he had a problem: he didn't know how to swim! Then, he remembered his Grandmother's instructions and started to sing the Toumkak song.

Out of nowhere, a gigantic snake swam up to him and said, "I heard you singing. You don't know how to swim, but I won't help you. You humans always hunt and eat us snakes!"

The little boy said, "King of all the snakes! Look at how big you are, and look at me. I am just a little boy. I don't even know yet how to boil a potato!"

Then, Ngata opened his bag and broke off a piece of cake and gave it to the snake. The snake ate it and said, "Wow! I didn't know that humans could be kind! Little boy, jump on my back."

"Little boy, you are different. Jump on my back!"

Ngata jumped on the back of the snake and was swiftly taken to the other side of the lake. The little boy gave thanks to the snake and continued his journey.

After several more days walking and searching, Ngata came to an enormous mountain of rocks. He had climbed little hills before, but never a mountain. Again, he started to sing the Toumkak song.

A mighty eagle flew down to him from a baobab tree and said, "Little boy, I heard you singing. You don't know how to climb, but I won't help you. You humans steal our eggs to make omelettes!"

The little boy said, "King of all the flying birds in the sky. Look at me. I'm just a little boy. I don't even know how to cook eggs!" Then, Ngata opened his bag, broke off a piece of cake, and gave it to the eagle. The bird ate it and said, "That was delicious! Little boy, you are different. Jump on my back!"

Ngata jumped on the back of the eagle and together they flew over the mountain. The little boy gave thanks to the eagle and continued his journey.

Ngata continued walking when suddenly he was upside down in a trap! He was surrounded by village people who came running at him with swords and spears. They were shouting to each other, and cut the strings of the trap to bring Ngata to the ground. Frightened, they dragged him into the village. When they arrived, there was music, drumming, and dancing. The King of the village was eating a big bloody chunk of meat. He stood up when he saw Ngata and there was complete silence. He demanded, "You, little boy, who sent you here?"

Ngata answered, "My Dad sent me to bring back the Toumkak that was stolen from my village."

The King laughed. Laughter echoed all around the village. Then, he raised his hands and said, "Silence! You are lucky that I just finished eating. Now, you will go and rest. Tomorrow, there will be a test. If you pass the test, you will go free. If you fail, you will be killed!" Then, there was music again.

They took Ngata to a room which was kept for prisoners, threw him inside, and locked the door. Before Ngata had a chance to cry, a dog snuck through a hole into the room. The dog looked like he hadn't eaten for days. Ngata opened his bag, broke off a piece of cake, and gave it to the dog. The dog took it, ate it, and said, "Thank you! No one here ever gives me anything." Then, he said, "Tomorrow morning, the King will have a dance, and all the girls will stand up to dance. The King will ask you which girl among all the girls is called Fanta. If you answer incorrectly, you will be killed." The little boy started to cry. The dog said, "Don't cry. Tomorrow, when all the girls are dancing and the King asks you the question, just start dancing with the girls. I will make my way there and rub up against Fanta." The little boy said thank you to the dog, and gave him another piece of cake. The dog disappeared into the night.

Ngata was about to lie down when a cat showed up. The little boy looked at the cat and felt pity, so he broke off a piece of cake and gave it to the cat. And the cat said, "I know why you are here. It is for your tribe's Toumkak. Listen, I just gave birth to seven kittens. I will bring them all here. Then, you will knock at the door and tell the guard that you can't sleep because we are making so much noise. They will have to take you to the next room, where all the stolen drums are kept. There, you will be close to your Toumkak." The boy said thank you to the cat, and the cat disappeared into the night.

Shortly after, a rat arrived in the room. The rat said, "I know why you are here." The boy opened his bag and gave a piece of cake to the rat. The rat ate the cake and said, "Thank you! I don't know why, but everybody here wants to kill me. Listen, when you go into the other room, I will come in the night and drop three seeds on one of the drums. The drum on which the seeds land will be your tribe's Toumkak." The little boy said thanks to the rat, and the rat disappeared.

The cat returned with her seven kittens. The little boy knocked at the door and the guard answered, "What is going on?" The little boy said, "I can't sleep! These cats are making a lot of noise." The King ordered, "Take him to the drum room and lock him inside there!"

So the guard took him out of the empty room and moved him over among the drums. The little boy's eyes were open the whole night, fearful. When it was almost morning, Ngata heard a noise and looked up to the roof. It was the rat! In the middle of the room, the rat dropped his three seeds, and they fell on a drum not too far from Ngata. That was the Toumkak! The stolen spiritual drum from Bazoula! Ngata couldn't wait for the King to send for him.

As the sun
began to rise, Ngata
heard the sound of
drums. There was
activity all over the village.
The King was already giving orders.
He called for the girls to start dancing, and
then he called the guard to bring the little boy.
The guard brought Ngata before the King.

The King said, "Little boy, you have one chance to save yourself. Among all these girls is one princess named Fanta. Go and show her to me." Ngata started to dance around with the girls. Finally, the dog arrived, made his way through the crowd and dancing girls, and started to rub against one girl. The boy chased the dog away, and started to dance with Fanta.

The music stopped. The King boomed, "Lucky boy, you found Fanta. Now, among the hundreds of drums we have stolen over the years, go choose the one that belongs to your tribe." The boy dashed into the room, grabbed the Toumkak, and started to make the call of his village on the drum:

crack dou kou, crack dou kou, crack dou kou, crack!
crack a brrack brrrack brrrack crack crack!

BOOOM!

Suddenly, he found himself in front of his house in Bazoula! He started to play the Toumkak again, and it reached the ears of everyone in the village. All the villagers came to see where the sound was coming from. When they arrived, they found the little boy playing the Toumkak. The whole village started to dance! Ngata's Dad ran away, never to be seen again. The King adopted Ngata and he became a prince. And when the King died, the little boy, by then a man, became the new King of Bazoula.

CONNECT IT

In the West African tradition, stories are often told with musical instruments and singing. Retell this story as a group. You may wish to divide parts of the story among group members. You may also wish to have other members provide music and sound effects.

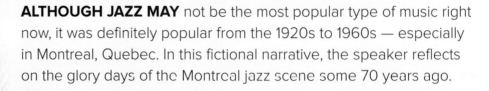

COOL MUSIC, HOT TOWN

ALTHOUGH JAZZ MAY not be the most popular type of music right now, it was definitely popular from the 1920s to 1960s — especially in Montreal, Quebec. In this fictional narrative, the speaker reflects on the glory days of the Montreal jazz scene some 70 years ago.

Kid, let me tell you the story about jazz in Montreal. Jazz has been in the fabric of Montreal in my life from the moment I was born. I live … jazz. I eat … jazz. I breathe … jazz. And like any jazz musician, you're always dreaming of that shining moment when you can play with the best of the best of them. Mmm, I can almost taste it.

Growing up in St. Henri, I was surrounded by music. My mother and sisters sang in the Union United Choir — the oldest Black church in Montreal. Oh boy, could they sing. And my uncle, my grand-uncle Brown, would always come by with his horn, showin' off, playing some old tune. He used to brag about his gig with the Canadian Ambassadors, Canada's hottest all-coloured orchestra.

My Daddy, he loved Canada. Came up from Harlem, got a job as a porter. And he would say, after riding trains all them years, that this is one beautiful country. He met my mother, a Scotian girl, right here in Montreal. Daddy loved going to the jazz shows. My mother didn't, though. She was a respectable lady, but she'd allow it. Perhaps because she saw how much joy it gave Daddy. She knew it wasn't easy for him to take orders from those white folks all day. He had to deal with all kinds of racism and prejudice.

Daddy'd gone to college back home for two years to become a dentist, but then the Depression got worse. He came to Montreal, 'cause he'd heard about it being freer from bigotry and Jim Crow. But there was no work in those days. No work for a coloured boy 'cept being a shoeshine boy or a porter, and, no, Black people still couldn't go to the clubs Uptown. So I think it wasn't much different for Daddy.

Know what I believe? I think he always wanted to be a drummer. He would tell me about the times he went to Café

St. Henri: *neighbourhood in southwestern Montreal*
coloured: *term that was used to refer to people of African descent; it is now considered offensive*
Jim Crow: *laws and customs enforcing racial segregation*

St. Michel, right across from Rockhead's. I memorized all the names of Louis Metcalf's International Band. I forget the names now — except for one … Herb Johnson on saxophone. And Daddy had an enormous record collection. Riding from town to town and sometimes into Chicago, he'd get the latest sides, but he always had a soft spot for Montreal jazz. He even got the first bebop record made in Canada by Wilk Wilkinson and the Boptet with … you guessed it, Herb Johnson on tenor sax.

But when was the first time I knew I wanted to be in music? Well … I must have been about 10 years old and I was taking lessons with Miss Daisy. Boy, how I hated to practise. But then Daddy put the radio on and I remember it clearly …

"Friends, you are all familiar with our six-foot-two, 18-year-old, now 19-year-old, coloured boy. Well, he's definitely taken Canada by storm as the greatest thing in barrelhouse, boogie-woogie, and beat me daddy eight to the bar since Mr. Steinway started making those pianos."

Isn't that something? I wanted to give that announcer a punch in his mouth. Not

OSCAR WAS CANADA'S FIRST INTERNATIONAL JAZZ STAR, AND HE BROKE THE COLOUR BARRIER.

Oscar Peterson. He was quick-witted, and he came back to that announcer. And when he played … woo. He could blow a fish out of the water. He was just a teenager, but Oscar could play with the best of 'em: Dizzy, Ella, Billie. Oscar was Canada's first international jazz star, and he broke the colour barrier. He risked his life playing in some places down south. He'd play with integrated bands and stay in coloured hotels with the lynch mob on his tail. And to think, I took lessons with his sister. I went to the same church he grew up in. He even came from St. Henri, just like me.

But I'll tell you what, the thing that stuck with me, what my dad said was, "Peetie, that's you. And what I mean is, you can make your dreams come true, just like Oscar. You can do anything, if you only put your mind to it and work real hard. They can take a lot of things from you but they can never take away your gift."

Then I said to my pops, "But Dad, didn't you want to be a dentist? How come you couldn't do that?"

And he said, "Son, you have opportunities that I didn't have. Now, make it happen." And this had a profound effect on me. Even at that age.

---

sides: *slang for records*

beat me daddy eight to the bar: *instruction to the rhythm section for eight beats, rather than four, to every bar of music*

integrated bands: *bands that included both Black and White musicians*

lynch mob: *group of people who want to kill someone without a trial*

Oscar Peterson

CONNECT IT

Rockhead's Paradise, the Union United Church, and Café St. Michel were important to the Montreal jazz scene because they were places where members of the Black community could go. Think of places where you like to go to feel safe. Why do you think it might be important for groups such as LGBT youth, people with disabilities, and people who are HIV-positive to have places where they can meet and feel safe?

All About Reggae

BY KLIVE WALKER

THINK ABOUT IT

What do you already know about reggae music? What else would you like to know?

REGGAE IS A popular type of music that originated in Jamaica during the 1960s. Bob Marley is credited with being reggae's first international superstar. He is responsible for spreading reggae around the world during the 1970s. But Jamaica's popular music did not start with reggae. It began many decades earlier. Read the following timeline to find out how the music of Jamaica spread throughout the world.

1930s to late 1950s
ORIGINS OF REGGAE

Calypso features a type of talk-singing about current events, jokes, and politics. A style similar to calypso is soca. Soca is a newer style of music that developed in the late 1960s and 1970s. Soca combines calypso and cadence (a genre from Dominica) with Indian musical instruments.

During this period, two types of music were very popular in Jamaica: jazz and mento. Jazz was created by African Americans and influenced by Caribbean rhythms. Jamaica produced its own exceptional jazz talent. Mento is a folk music, but it is sometimes described as Jamaican calypso. Louise Bennett, the godmother of Jamaican folklore, was a mento singer and recording artist.

In the 1950s, when calypso experienced significant international popularity, Jamaican mento performers were often grouped with calypso music. Harry Belafonte, a Jamaican American film star and folksinger, was the first solo recording artist to sell a million records. His successful 1956 album is called *Calypso*, even though it is a collection of mento and folk songs. Bennett was one of Belafonte's greatest influences.

Around the same time, a hand-drumming genre called *nyabinghi* became popular. It became associated with Rastafari, a spiritual and cultural way of life based on African Jamaican culture.

The Skatalites give a concert in Hamburg, Germany.

Late 1950s to 1960s

SKA

In the late 1950s, jazz, mento, and nyabinghi had combined with R&B and Latin music to make ska, a unique Jamaican sound. For hundreds of years, Jamaica had been a colony of Britain. In 1962, Jamaica became independent from Britain, and could elect its own government. Ska became the first popular music of an independent Jamaica.

The Skatalites band were the main stars of ska. Most of their songs were instrumentals featuring solos by their brass section. Don Drummond was the band's trombonist. He had a magnetic presence and was considered a genius on his instrument.

In the late 1970s, there was a ska revival in the United Kingdom. British ska bands copied the music of their Jamaican heroes. In the early 1980s, British ska started to influence Canadian and American music.

1960s to 1980s

REGGAE IN CANADA

In the 1960s, many Jamaicans were immigrating to Canada. Musicians were among them. Pianist Jackie Mittoo, trumpet player Jo Jo Bennett, and singers Jay Douglas and Leroy Sibbles are some of the pioneers of Jamaican Canadian music. They all established music careers in their new home. During the late 1970s and 1980s, musicians with roots in Jamaica and other Caribbean nations developed roots reggae, a style of reggae that was rooted in their Canadian experience.

The words of their songs spoke about Toronto neighbourhoods, racism, women's rights, the environment, and equality.

Roots reggae still has a big presence in Canada. Although Toronto seems to be Canada's reggae hotspot, that status is being challenged. There are major reggae festivals in Montreal and Calgary. There are also major artists. Vancouver DJ Jahranimo and Edmonton roots reggae band Souljah Fyah are just two examples.

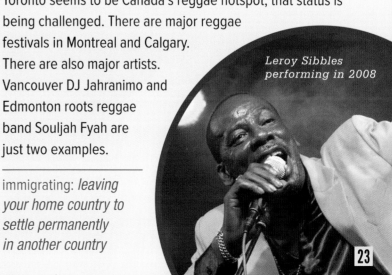

Leroy Sibbles performing in 2008

immigrating: *leaving your home country to settle permanently in another country*

23

The Heptones, a Jamaican rocksteady and reggae vocal trio

1966 to 1968
ROCKSTEADY

1968 to 1980
ROOTS REGGAE

A new music known as rocksteady emerged in 1966. It had a slower, more relaxed sound than ska. Its lyrics often talked about romance and justice.

The shift to roots reggae began in 1968 and the early 1970s. The music's basslines were similar to rocksteady, but the drums played a rhythm called the "one drop." The guitar and keyboards were played in a percussive way. The lyrics spoke of equality, justice, Rastafari, romance, African pride, and global African heritage. Reggae is not just music. Reggae is a culture whose rhythms have influenced poetry, theatre, film, art, and fashion.

percussive: *like drums*

Judy Mowatt, a Jamaican reggae artist and vocalist for Bob Marley

An influential dancehall artist, Sugar Minott, 29 June 1985

1970 to 1980s

DUB

1980s to 1990s

DANCEHALL

Dub strips an existing roots reggae song down to its drum and bass parts. Reverb, echo, and pauses are then added. Sometimes, snippets of brass instruments and singing from the original song are put back into the mix. Dub is a genre where producers and studio engineers are the stars. Since the 1970s, dub-like reggae has become a building block for music around the world.

Dub poetry has strong roots in Canada. Dub poets craft poems so that when they are spoken without music, the listener can hear a reggae rhythm in the words. Lillian Allen is one of the pioneers of this type of reggae poetry.

Reverb: *sound repeated several times, similar to an echo*

Lee "Scratch" Perry is an innovative Jamaican producer. Perry was one of the pioneers of dub music.

Dancehall was first used to describe outdoor parties in 1950s Jamaica. It was at these parties that vinyl records were played on huge speaker systems. The person who played the records was called the "selector." The person introducing the music was the "toaster," later known as a DJ. By the late 1960s, DJs became recording artists on their own. This genre became known as dancehall in the early 1980s. The dancehall sound is upbeat and exciting. Although there are dancehall singers, this music is known for its DJs.

In the late 1980s and 1990s, dancehall ruled most of the reggae world. Canada had only a few dancehall stars during this time, such as DJ Carla Marshall. Most Canadian MCs of Caribbean heritage decided to express their reggae influences through hip hop.

MCs: *people who provide entertainment by instructing DJs and rapping*

CONNECT IT

Go online and research a music style that is not mentioned in this timeline. Write a short fact card that could be added to this timeline.

CANADIAN HIP-HOP WALL OF FAME

Who are some Canadian hip-hop artists that you listen to? What do you like about them?

DID YOU KNOW that some people credit DJ Kool Herc's 1973 basement parties as the start of modern hip hop? At these parties, Kool Herc began mixing breakbeats with "toasting." Toasting involves talking over music. Toasting has roots in Jamaican music and African storytelling. Soon, Kool Herc's parties were so popular that they were moved to clubs. From there, the music of hip hop was born.

In the early days of hip hop, the genre was usually referred to as rap. During this time, hip hop was played only on the streets, at parties, in clubs, and on certain radio stations. Hip-hop music has come a long way since then. Check out this wall of fame to learn about some of the history of Canada's hip-hop scene.

breakbeats: *short repeated phrases (e.g., drum solos) that are looped using turntables*

SONGS

First Canadian Mainstream Hip-Hop Hit

"MY DEFINITION OF A BOOMBASTIC JAZZ STYLE"

This 1990 hit by the Dream Warriors had international success.

Capital Q (Frank Allert) and King Lou (Louis Robinson) of the Canadian rap group the Dream Warriors

CHART-TOPPERS

Rapper With the Most #1 Hits

DRAKE

In 2012, Toronto's Drake beat Jay Z for the most #1 hits on the Billboard R&B/Hip-Hop charts. At the time, Jay Z had nine hits and Drake had just scored his 10th.

First French-Language Hip-Hop Group With a Single on Canada's Francophone Charts

DUBMATIQUE

After forming in 1997, Montreal's Dubmatique found success in both English- and French-speaking regions.

First Canadian Rapper to Have a US Top 40 Hit

MAESTRO FRESH WES

In 1989, Maestro Fresh Wes (a.k.a. Maestro) broke into the US Top 40 charts with "Let Your Backbone Slide." This song remained the bestselling Canadian hip-hop single until 2008.

How much do you know about Canadian hip-hop artists compared to American ones? Why do you think that is the case?

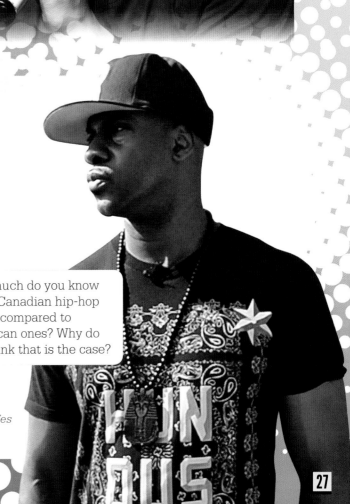

Maestro Fresh Wes

BREAKTHROUGHS

Greatest Dream-Come-True Story

WONDAGURL

When this Brampton-based teen sent her song to rapper Travis Scott, she didn't know that it would change her life. At the time, Scott was in the studio with Jay Z. Jay Z later included WondaGurl's beats on his 2013 *Magna Carta... Holy Grail* album.

First Prominent Canadian Female Rapper

MICHIE MEE

Jamaican-born Michie Mee, who started her career in the late 1980s, is known as "Canada's hip-hop queen."

First Canadian Rap Group Signed to a Major Label

MCJ AND COOL G

This Halifax hip-hop duo signed a deal with Capitol Records in 1989.

First Rapper to Be Named a Poet Laureate

CADENCE WEAPON

This Alberta rap artist was named Edmonton's poet laureate in 2009.

Mood Ruff members perform at Peg City Holla 2003 in Winnipeg.

First Major Hip-Hop Group From Winnipeg

MOOD RUFF

This group formed in 1994 and included members Spitz, Odario, Breakz, and ICQRI.

Canada's First Hip-Hop Radio Program

THE FANTASTIC VOYAGE

In 1983, this radio show created by DJ Ron Nelson was played on Ryerson University's radio station CKLN 89.5 FM.

Most Genre Crossing in Canadian Hip Hop

K-OS

Toronto musician k-os has used genres like rap, R&B, rock, rockabilly, reggae, ska, folk, country, and blues as inspiration for his songs.

Youngest Canadian Female Rapper Signed to a Major Label

REEMA MAJOR

At just 16 years old, Sudanese-born Toronto rapper Reema Major signed a worldwide record deal in 2010.

ONSCREEN

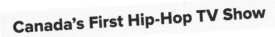

Canada's First Hip-Hop TV Show

RAPCITY

Beginning in 1989 on MuchMusic, *RapCity* was first hosted by Michael Williams.

First Canadian Rap Documentary

MAKE SOME NOISE (1994)

Runner-Up: *Raisin' Kane: A Rapumentary* (2000)

Canada's First Hip-Hop TV Drama

DROP THE BEAT

After premiering on CBC in 2000, the series was praised for showing the reality of the 1990s Canadian hip-hop scene.

First Internationally Acclaimed Canadian Hip-Hop Music Video Director

DIRECTOR X

Toronto-born Director X has worked with several big-name stars. Some of those stars include Rihanna, LL Cool J, Alicia Keys, Usher, and Jay Z.

CONNECT IT

Research a hip-hop act from this selection that you have not listened to before. Write a short biography about the act. Share your biography and a sample of the artist's music with your classmates.

LET'S HEAR IT!

What are some of the challenges musicians might face when trying to break into the music scene?

READ THESE SHORT REPORTS to find out how these artists and organizations were able to break out and bring their music to the masses.

CLASSICAL

Classical contralto Portia White was the first African Canadian concert singer who had international success. She was born in Truro, Nova Scotia, in 1911. At six years old, White started singing in the church choir. To get to her weekly music lessons, White would walk 16 kilometres. It was her dream of becoming a professional singer that kept her going. Although there was an audience for classical singing, barriers were placed in her way because she was Black.

Despite racial barriers, White made her national debut in Toronto in 1941 and her international debut in New York in 1944. In 1952, a vocal injury forced White to stop performing. After her injury, White became a teacher and she taught until she died in 1968. Very few of her recordings exist today. In 1995, the Government of Canada named Portia White a "person of national historic significance."

contralto: *type of female classical singer who sings the lowest part in opera and classical music*

Portia White

URBAN MUSIC

Urban music includes genres like soul, R&B, rap, dance, reggae, blues, and gospel. For many years, people tried to get urban music on Canadian radio. They had their applications to the Canadian Radio-Television Telecommunications Commission (CRTC) repeatedly turned down. Luckily, there were pioneers who helped support urban music.

Tony Young, better known as Master T, exposed Canada to the urban music scene. In the early 1990s, Master T played urban music on MuchMusic TV shows *RapCity* and *X-Tendamix*. In 1991, the musical group Dance Appeal was formed to show support for Canadian urban radio stations. In 1996, the Urban Music Association of Canada (UMAC) was formed to promote Canadian urban music. In 2001, the CRTC finally allowed Flow 93.5 FM, Canada's first urban music station, to air.

Over the next few years, many Canadian cities got their own urban radio stations. More and more urban radio stations are being added every year, including the recent creation of G98.7 FM in Toronto.

Tony Young (Master T)

R&B

Some of Canada's R&B singers have been told that there is no audience for their type of music in Canada. Somali Canadian singer Al Spx was advised to go to the United Kingdom to become a star. Now she plays to sold-out audiences all over Europe.

Canadian R&B singers often have just as much success in the United States as they do in Canada — sometimes they have more. Artists like this include Tamia, Melanie Fiona, Deborah Cox, and Glenn Lewis. Cox won an American Soul Train Award in 1999 for her song "Nobody's Supposed to Be Here." Fiona won Best New Artist at the Soul Train Music Awards in 2010 and two Grammy Awards in 2012. Other artists with success in the United States include Kreesha Turner and Keshia Chanté. Both have had their music played on television and radio stations in Canada and the United States. Others like Melanie Durrant, Divine Brown, Love & Sas, and In Essence have also put Canadian R&B on the map.

Keshia Chanté

Jully Black poses with her Juno Award in 2008.

R&B CONTINUED

Jully Black is another example of homegrown R&B talent. She says, "After touring our beautiful country … I have concluded that the citizens of Canada LOVE them some R&B soul music. … The only problem is, unless they are spoon-fed this music by those who have the influence … they [think] that a lot of us Canadian R&B soul singers have stopped making music. … This is when Canada runs the risk of losing even more of our great Canadian musical gems … [because there isn't] a true home or platform for the music to be heard."

A DAY IN THE LIFE OF
JULLY BLACK

8–9 a.m.	Wake up, devotion, pray, get ready for the day
9–11 a.m.	Yoga or workout; drink my breakfast shake
11–12 p.m.	Shower, check email, post to my fans on social media
12–1 p.m.	Lunch; read spiritually uplifting book
1–2 p.m.	Voice lesson (three times a week); talk to my business partner, drummer, producer, musical director (news of the day, updates); call Mom
2–4 p.m.	Creative time! Singing by myself, songwriting work with guitar, listening to influences, watching old videos of singers I look up to (e.g., Tina Turner, Etta James, Whitney Houston)
4–5 p.m.	Listen to my preachers or something inspirational that will feed my soul; eat
5–7 p.m.	Yoga class or workout
7–8 p.m.	Conference with JBE (Jully Black Entertainment team) because some are in different time zones
8–9 p.m.	Guitar time (usually go for 30 minutes of practising) with my guitar buddy (guitar lesson on Sundays)
9–10 p.m.	Watch online shows for fun
10–11 p.m.	Go to studio to record
11–12 a.m.	Make green tea with honey and lemon; call Mom and catch up
12–1 a.m.	Go to bed

CONNECT IT

Design a poster to promote Canadian talent featuring one of the artists or radio stations mentioned in this article.

Dear Abiola

THINK ABOUT IT

If you had a problem, would you consider writing to an advice columnist? Why or why not?

DO YOU HAVE problems? If so, today's your lucky day! Fictional advice columnist Abiola Okinedo is here to answer your questions.

Dear Abiola,

I've been a fan of hip hop for as long as I can remember. I started writing my own raps in grade 2. The problem is that, in my parents' eyes, rap is offensive. Even though I'm a good kid with good grades, they think rap is a bad influence. I really want to try being a rapper, and I think I'm pretty good at it. I know my parents won't understand. What should I do?

From,
Strictly Rap

Hey, Strictly Rap.

You've come to the right place. I know all about strict parents. I'd suggest you sit your parents down and say, "Mom and Dad, I want to be a rapper." But before you do that, you need some strong arguments to convince them it's a good idea. Remind them that you're a good kid with good grades. You might even want to show them that there are a lot of positive rappers out there, like KRS-One, Mos Def, k-os, and Shad. They use music as a way to express their feelings about social, cultural, and political issues.

Good luck!
Abiola

Dear Abiola,

I go to a school in a big city in British Columbia and we don't have music classes. I know kids at other schools who get to play musical instruments. Some even get to play in a band and go on tour. That would be really cool. It's not fair!

Thanks!
Out of Tune

Dear Out of Tune,

It's time to take action! Start by talking to your teachers, principal, or other adults so they know this issue is important to you. Then you could start a petition or write a letter to your school board trustees. You can also research organizations that grant money for schools to buy musical instruments. Or try raising some money yourself. If none of that works, some community centres offer free music lessons to kids. There are also organizations like MusiCounts that are working to make sure kids everywhere get the chance to make music.

Abiola

Shad

CONNECT IT

With a partner, create your own advice column about school. What types of questions would you most like to answer? Who would answer the questions? Come up with two sample questions and answers and share your work with another pair.

Singing for RIGHTS

Tiki Mercury-Clarke

THINK ABOUT IT

What songs do you know with a positive message? Choose an inspiring lyric, phrase, or stanza from this song and share it with a partner. Tell your partner what makes the song powerful.

SONGS CAN MOVE us to action. The American Civil Rights Movement was a period during the 1950s and 1960s in which African Americans protested for their equal rights. In this article, you'll read about how the American Civil Rights Movement affected people in Canada. You'll also read about the important role music played.

When footage from the American Civil Rights Movement reached television sets, people all over the world could see what was happening. For Tiki Mercury-Clarke, the images of people standing up for their rights were very significant. She experienced a lot of racism while growing up in Toronto during the 1950s and 1960s.

"What happened in the US, the impact it had on us in Toronto, was great. It was a great source of encouragement to me and strength for me," she says. Mercury-Clarke is a performing artist, song stylist, educator, storyteller, and pianist. She sings gospel songs and songs about justice, many of which come from old spirituals sung in the United States.

spirituals: *songs that came out of the African American musical tradition. They often had encoded messages and were sung by enslaved Africans to convey secret messages about escaping.*

When she was nine years old, Mercury-Clarke and her family moved to an all-White neighbourhood in Toronto. Her grandfather was a Caribbean American who came to Toronto after serving time in jail for speaking out against the involvement of Africans in World War I. Things were not easy for Mercury-Clarke in her new community. When she and her brother walked home from school, they were called names by White parents and children. They were even spat on and had things thrown at them.

The images of the American Civil Rights Movement on television, along with her encouraging grandparents, helped Mercury-Clarke.

"When every heart joins every heart and together yearns for liberty, that's when we'll be free."

"When I was being attacked by the parents and kids walking up Simpson Avenue, it was the same thing as escaping the Underground Railroad. One of the things that kept me going was that I wasn't alone. I could see what other children were going through … in the United States," said Mercury-Clarke.

One thing that helped people in the United States fight for their rights was music. The 2009 documentary *Soundtrack for a Revolution* tells the story of the American Civil Rights Movement through music. The documentary takes viewers to picket lines and jail cells. It shows that even when civil rights activists, both Black and White, were being beaten, assaulted, or jailed, they would sing songs to affirm their unity and give them strength. Singing these songs, which were sometimes called spirituals, helped people feel connected to their ancestors.

"Spirituals in particular were always about freedom. Freedom to move. Freedom to express. Freedom to sing. Freedom to create," says Karen Burke. In 1988, Burke co-founded the Toronto Mass Choir, a gospel choir. Currently, she teaches in the Faculty of Fine Arts at York University.

One song that was sung in the United States during the Civil Rights Movement was "The Hymn to Freedom" by Oscar Peterson, who was born in Montreal in 1925. The song lyrics, written by Harriette Hamilton, say, "When every heart joins every heart and together yearns for liberty, that's when we'll be free."

When writing the song, Peterson thought back to the spirituals he grew up with. He thought about Martin Luther King Jr. and the Civil Rights Movement taking place. After the song's release, he began receiving phone calls from the United States and Europe. The phone calls let him know that his song was being sung in various places as an anthem to the Civil Rights Movement.

Music has played an essential role in other social movements throughout history. During slavery, enslaved African Americans sang songs like "Follow the Drinking Gourd," which had encoded messages for escape to Canada through the Underground Railroad. More recently, the music of Black South Africans was a rallying cry during the anti-Apartheid movement of the last half of the 20th century.

CONNECT IT

Imagine you were an activist in the American Civil Rights Movement. Write a journal entry about the importance of music in your life. Use information found in this report and your own research.

MUSIC by Prudence

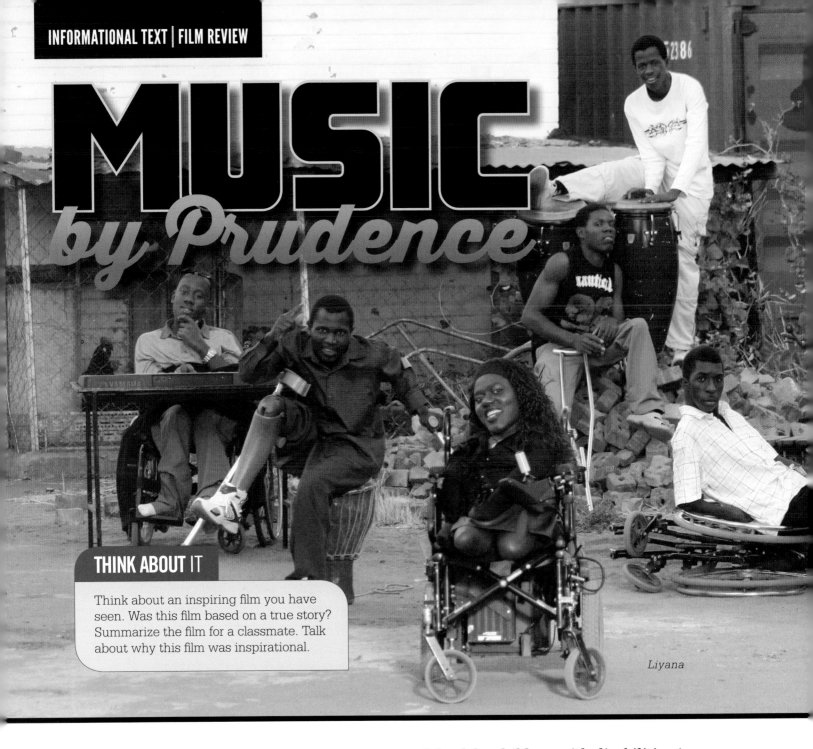

THINK ABOUT IT

Think about an inspiring film you have seen. Was this film based on a true story? Summarize the film for a classmate. Talk about why this film was inspirational.

Liyana

IN THIS FILM REVIEW, you'll read all about the band Liyana and one of its lead vocalists, Prudence Mabhena.

Imagine making a film in a country "with sporadic electricity, water, and basic resources." This is exactly what some talented filmmakers did. *Music by Prudence* features musicians with physical disabilities living in Zimbabwe. It won the 2010 Academy Award for Best Documentary (Short Subject).

Music by Prudence opens with one of the lead vocalists, Prudence Mabhena, calling out the word "Liyana" to the other band members. She spent time at King George VI School for children with disabilities (or KGVI as it's called for short). She has two dreams: "Being able to sing for thousands and thousands of people" and "being able to be independent." Through these dreams, the story of Liyana unfolds.

The film gives viewers a slice of life in Zimbabwe. The distant mountains, red dirt, panoramic sky, flat lands, birds chirping, and the bell of a cow set the scene. Life in Zimbabwe isn't just picturesque. There are hardships, too. In this documentary, Liyana uses its meaningful songs to show the challenges of growing up with a disability in Zimbabwe.

sporadic: *with interruptions*

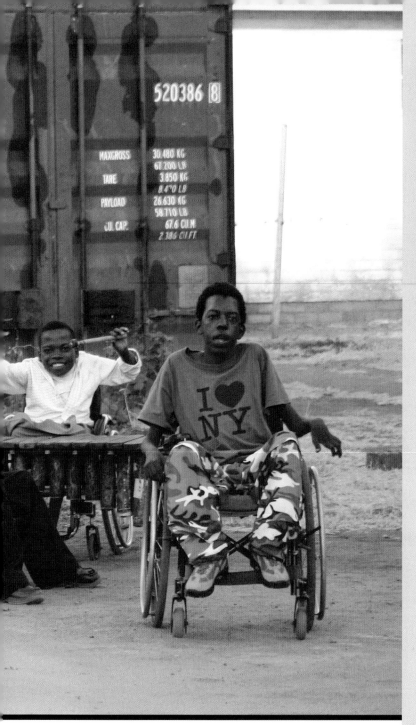

BERNIE PITTERS

Another artist who has achieved his dreams despite the odds is reggae keyboardist Bernie Pitters. Pitters has played professionally all over the world. He was the keyboardist for the band Toots and the Maytals for 10 years. In this interview, he talks about barriers he has faced because of his disability.

Born: England, grew up in Jamaica, immigrated to Canada in 1976

Have you always been blind?
My vision started to decline in 1988. That's when I had to resign from my international touring with Toots and the Maytals.

What caused your blindness?
It was a side effect of diabetes … I did eight to 12 laser surgeries and three rectractomies. I shouldn't have gone on tour right away. When you have those surgeries, you're not supposed to do heavy lifting. The surgeries didn't heal.

Why did you have to stop touring?
It was a management decision. Toots was mainly a visual show. We used to do a split across the stage and I had to manually do it with the keyboard. I would miss all of those shots. You had to know the song and watch his hand movements. I couldn't keep up with it.

Did playing music become more of a challenge?
Yes, because I [had to refuse] to take on certain projects. I have to memorize properly what I am doing and play by memory.

Did you learn to read Braille?
I tried to but, as a keyboard player, there are callouses on my fingertips. So it's very hard for me to recognize Braille … the technology is advanced now, so we have Braille readers and other kinds of readers. I am using a program called JAWS, which reads from the computer for me.

How do you make up for not seeing?
Hearing. My hearing is so intense. Things sound extremely loud to me and I got to know what it is and identify it … So when things are really loud and everything is coming at you, it's an extreme high pressure. You have to learn patience.

Viewers of this film can't help but notice the joy expressed on the faces of members of Liyana when they perform. This is the case whether Liyana is performing in local communities, rehearsing at KGVI, or performing on the stage at the Bulawayo Theatre. Each band member has a disability, such as hearing impairment, muscular dystrophy, or spina bifida.

Liyana's songs provide the soundtrack to the movie. They range from the Kiswahili song "Malaika," which means angel, to the Afro-fusion tune "Going Nowhere." The music is the thread that brings the story together. *Music by Prudence* inspires viewers to dream impossible dreams despite the odds.

CONNECT IT

Go online and research other musicians who have disabilities. Write a fact card about this musician. What kind of music does he or she play? What are some of his or her accomplishments? Share your fact card with a partner.

Faith Nolan
SINGING FOR CHANGE

THINK ABOUT IT

What is something you believe in that you would stand up for? Brainstorm creative ways you can have your voice heard through music.

FAITH NOLAN IS a musician with a lot of talent. She also has a lot of heart! Read all about her in this profile.

Africville was Halifax's oldest and largest Black community. Many of its residents were descendants of Black Loyalists and War of 1812 Black Refugees. At its largest, Africville had 400 Black residents. The community had a school and churches. However, residents did not have the same access to clean drinking water, proper roads, or electricity as the people of Halifax. In the 1960s, the Halifax government began to demolish Africville. The mayor of Halifax issued an apology to the former residents and their descendants in 2010 for the conditions they endured when they lived in Africville.

When walking through the hallways of one of Ontario's largest correctional facilities, the last thing you might expect to hear is a guitar strumming the blues and bright voices singing along. Enter Faith Nolan. For the past 30 years, this Canadian folk and roots singer has been leading songwriting workshops for women in jail.

Nolan was born in 1957 in Africville, just outside Halifax, Nova Scotia. Her father was of African and Mi'kmaq heritage. He died when she was only seven. Nolan, her mother, and her sister moved to the Regent Park area of Toronto when she was four. This was around the same time that the government began demolishing the homes, schools, and historic church of Africville. In the 1970s, Nolan began performing. She has recorded over 10 albums. Today, she lives in Toronto with her partner and two dogs.

Nolan began visiting prison when two female cousins were imprisoned for murder. She would sing to them. Then, she began getting calls to return to share her songs with other inmates.

Mi'kmaq: *First Nations with traditional lands in the Maritime provinces, parts of Quebec, and parts of New England in the United States*

> *"Music is a universal language, and love is the key."*

Like many of the inmates she works with, Nolan has experienced being poor. As well, she has mixed First Nations and African heritage, two groups that are overrepresented in the prison system. Music has helped her deal with many difficult moments. "The sound ... the repetition ... it's very calming," she says.

Growing up, Nolan was exposed to many types of music. Her musical roots extend on both sides of her family — Irish and African Nova Scotian. She has memories of her late father playing jazz guitar, her mother on the drums, in a band. Celtic-influenced East Coast tunes, spirituals from the Baptist church in Africville, soul, calypso, and gospel were the soundscape of her early childhood.

Nolan was inspired by civil rights activists, including Angela Davis and the late Nelson Mandela. An artist who was one of her biggest influences was Odetta. Odetta was known as "the voice of the Civil Rights Movement." She was a songwriter who played guitar and helped revive the American folk movement. Nolan had the chance to play with Odetta before Odetta died in 2008.

Songs come naturally to Nolan, who taught herself the guitar as well as the banjo, ukulele, harp, harmonica, bass, and drums.

"Music is just something you did," she says about becoming a musician. Yet there is nothing accidental about the blend of folk, blues, and roots in Nolan's protest songs. Nolan's songs speak out about important issues such as poverty, AIDS, and human rights in Canada and around the world.

Nolan believes strongly in rights for prisoners. On her album *Jailhouse Blues*, she helped give a voice to thousands of women who are locked away from their families and communities.

"Music is a universal language, and love is the key," she says.

CONNECT IT

Africville was a Black community that did not have the same services as other communities. Imagine you lived in Africville. Write a letter to a politician about the conditions in your community and why they were unfair.

KNOW THE BIZ

CAREERS IN THE
MUSIC INDUSTRY

THINK ABOUT IT

Imagine a career you would like to have when you grow up. Write a list of skills you would need for this career.

MUSIC IS NOT only a part of everyday life. It can also be part of an exciting career. Read the following fact cards to find out how these music lovers turned their passion into a career.

My life as ... A JAZZ SINGER

NAME: Kellylee Evans

HOMETOWN: Scarborough, Ontario

EDUCATION:
- Bachelor of Arts in English Literature (Carleton University)
- Bachelor of Arts in Legal Studies (Carleton University)

JOB DESCRIPTION: "[My job involves] performing and recording music for people around the world."

WHAT DO YOU LIKE MOST ABOUT YOUR CAREER?
"Getting to interact with the audiences and musicians. It's a career where I am surrounded by people that I love. I especially love the impact that music and our concerts have on audiences. People leave our concerts happy."

WHAT ARE SOME CHALLENGES OF YOUR CAREER?
"I really don't see my career as having challenges. I have personal challenges that I have to overcome. [These include] staying positive and having faith, working hard and working smart, accepting help, and following my instinct. Once I conquer those challenges, all goes well."

Kellylee Evans performing at the Beaches International Jazz Festival, Toronto

DJ L'Oqenz

Eboué "Eb" Talivaldis Tihai Reinbergs

My life as ... A DJ

NAME: DJ L'Oqenz (pronounced eloquence)

HOMETOWN: Toronto, Ontario

EDUCATION: Completed high school and went straight into her profession

JOB DESCRIPTION: "As a DJ, my job is to create blends and mixes. ... [I also] educate the listener through my musical selections. No matter what the event, I always aim to educate and evoke feeling. Dancing is also a good sign that I'm doing my job well!"

WHAT DO YOU LIKE MOST ABOUT YOUR CAREER? "I enjoy music, creating, travelling, and meeting new people in my career."

WHAT ARE SOME CHALLENGES OF YOUR CAREER? "Challenges include the late hours and juggling my schedule between being a DJ and being a mother."

My life as ... A MUSIC AND ENTERTAINMENT LAWYER

NAME: Eboué "Eb" Talivaldis Tihai Reinbergs

HOMETOWN: Dar es Salaam, Tanzania

EDUCATION:
• Bachelor of Commerce and Finance (University of Toronto)
• Master of Business Administration (MBA) (York University)
• Bachelor of Laws (University of Windsor)
• Juris Doctor (University of Detroit Mercy), licensed to practise law in the Province of Ontario and the State of New York

JOB DESCRIPTION: "Entertainment lawyers are DEAL MAKERS. I negotiate deals on behalf of my clients, and then I prepare paperwork to reflect the deal that has been made."

WHAT DO YOU LIKE MOST ABOUT YOUR CAREER? "Working with musicians and other talented artists is fun for me. I wouldn't change it for anything."

WHAT ARE SOME CHALLENGES OF YOUR CAREER? "When you're good at something people will always demand your time. ... It is important to plan your time [well] or you may not accomplish your goals."

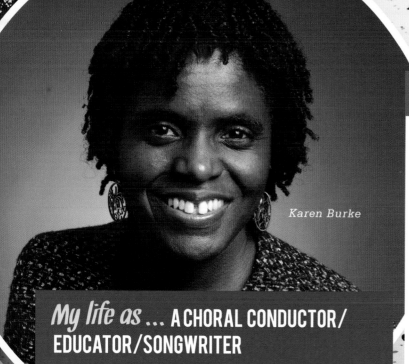
Karen Burke

My life as ... A CHORAL CONDUCTOR/EDUCATOR/SONGWRITER

NAME: Karen Burke

HOMETOWN: Brantford, Ontario

EDUCATION:
- Bachelor of Music (McMaster University)
- Associate of The Royal Conservatory of Music (ARCT) diploma in Piano Teaching

JOB DESCRIPTION: "Here at York, I am Associate Professor of Music with a main portfolio of gospel music and music education. With Toronto Mass Choir, I am the principal director. I guess I am the booking agent, too. I am also a workshop clinician. So I am asked to go work in a lot of different places with educational institutions, universities, schools, festivals, organizations, choirs, and also different countries to do gospel music workshops."

WHAT DO YOU LIKE MOST ABOUT YOUR CAREER? "I like the fact that no day is ever the same. It brings me into contact with people from a lot of different walks of life, which I really enjoy. [I also love] meeting different people and being able to share music with them. I love the fact that I get to travel, and love to make choirs out of people who are unsuspecting."

WHAT ARE SOME CHALLENGES OF YOUR CAREER? "It gets really busy sometimes. There are periods that get really, really busy and then you have your periods when you have to relax. So I think I haven't quite found that balance yet. But I do enjoy my work and I think it is a privilege to find work that you enjoy."

My life as ... A MUSIC JOURNALIST

NAME: Del F. Cowie

HOMETOWN: Bristol, England

EDUCATION: Honours Mass Communications/Sociology (York University)

JOB DESCRIPTION: Music writer and associate editor of *Exclaim!* magazine

WHAT DO YOU LIKE MOST ABOUT YOUR CAREER? "I enjoy the fact that I get a chance to write about music and popular culture. In my writing, I often relate music and pop culture to history."

WHAT ARE SOME CHALLENGES OF YOUR CAREER? "The challenge — that I find that remains constant and needs to be embraced — is remaining versatile and adaptable. This means being open to change and learning new skills while balancing your interests and goals."

Del F. Cowie

CONNECT IT

Summarize what you've read in this piece by creating a "help wanted advertisement" for one of these careers. Review real advertisements online or in a newspaper before creating your own.

ROCK ON!

THINK ABOUT IT

Have you ever liked something that was unpopular with your friends? How did it make you feel?

DO YOU LIKE rock music? If so, this report is for you.

Black musicians have been rocking out for generations. Way back in the 1950s, groundbreaking rock and rollers like Chuck Berry, Little Richard, Bo Diddley, and Fats Domino paved the way for other rock acts. These earlier musicians drew on African American R&B and soul music traditions.

Rock and roll music was, and still is, loud and communicates raw emotions. Rock musicians combine the sounds of instruments like pianos and electric guitars. In the 1960s, it was psychedelic rocker Jimi Hendrix who took guitar playing to the next level. You might not know it, but Jimi Hendrix had a Canadian connection. His grandmother and grandfather, Nora and Ross Hendrix, lived in a Black neighbourhood in Vancouver, British Columbia, called Hogan's Alley. Hendrix spent much of his childhood there, and he even lived there for a period of time after he served in the United States Army. Today, there's a Jimi Hendrix shrine in what was once Hogan's Alley.

In 1958, around the same time Hendrix picked up his first guitar, Tina Turner first hit the stage. She's been inspiring rockers ever since.

These pioneers inspired many others to continue the rock tradition, including Prince and Lenny Kravitz. In 1990, the rock band Living Colour was given the first Grammy Award for Best Hard Rock Performance. They won the award in 1991, too.

Another important part of history is the Afropunk movement, which is made up of Black people in the punk rock and alternative music scenes. In 1993, African American filmmaker James Spooner made a film called *Afro-Punk* that explores what it means to be Black in these traditionally White music scenes. In 2002, the first annual Afropunk festival was hosted in Brooklyn, New York. Unlocking the Truth, a three-member heavy metal band based in Brooklyn, New York, proves that kids can rock, too. The band performed at the Afropunk festival in 2012 as well as on various television shows.

One thing's for sure — Canadians know how to rock, too. In Toronto, Washington Savage gathered a group of musicians in the 1990s to form the band Blaxam, which included guitarist Adrian X, who went on to perform with artists like Drake.

"I grew up playing in a rock 'n' roll band," said Adrian X in an interview. "My best friends and I had a band since we were 13. We listened to all the amazing bands like Hendrix, Led Zeppelin, the Police, Fishbone, 24/7 Spyz, Living Colour. We also listened to lots of jazz and blues. I was surrounded by music."

Today, Canadian rockers are still taking to the stage. Among them are Danko Jones, Fefe Dobson, Saidah Baba Talibah, the OBGMs, and Murray Lightburn, lead singer of the indie rock band the Dears.

Danko Jones may have summed up the catchiness of rock music best when he said, "I knew I loved rock the moment I heard it!"

CONNECT IT

Write a list of five adjectives that describe rock and roll music. Use these five adjectives in a persuasive paragraph that argues why you like or dislike this genre of music.

MUSICIANS WHO GIVE BACK

THINK ABOUT IT

Do you think musicians have a responsibility to give back to their communities? Why or why not?

In these fact cards, you'll learn about talented artists who aren't just great musicians. They're great people, too.

JULLY BLACK

Name: Jully Black

Occupation: Singer and songwriter

Born in: Toronto, Ontario

Organization: CARE Canada, an organization that empowers women and girls in the fight against global poverty

What does she do? As the organization's Ambassador of Change, Black helps raise awareness about CARE Canada.

She says: "I have many platforms [as Ambassador of Change], but the one that resonates most is the education of girls and women in developing countries. It's been proven that when girls are educated everybody wins. ... We [also] need to make a difference here in Canada. [We need to] not to take education for granted and [prove] that girls can learn, too. ... It is very important for those of us who are given the platform ... [and] voice, to lend them to our organizations. ... I believe we were put on this earth to serve one another."

ALICIA KEYS

Name: Alicia Keys

Occupation: R&B singer

Born in: New York, New York

Organization: Co-founder and Global Ambassador of Keep a Child Alive, a non-profit that puts medicine in the hands of families living with HIV and AIDS in Africa

What does she do? Keys organizes the Black Ball, an annual fundraiser for her Keep a Child Alive organization. She also works year-round to bring awareness to the issue of childhood AIDS in Africa.

She says: "There is no age requirement for making a difference … We all hold unlimited power and we should use it!"

KARDINAL OFFISHALL

Name: Kardinal Offishall

Occupation: Rapper

Born in: Scarborough, Ontario

Organizations: Annual Fundraiser for the Hospital for Sick Children (also known as SickKids) and Free the Children, One by One

What does he do? Kardinal Offishall works to bring awareness to children's issues around the world. He hosts an annual fundraiser for SickKids, and has hosted events for Free the Children.

He says: "It doesn't really take a lot from one person. If everybody chipped in and just played their part … that force is immeasurable."

GILBERTO GIL

Name: Gilberto Gil

Occupation: Singer and songwriter, guitarist, activist, former Brazilian Minister of Culture (2003–2008)

Born in: Salvador de Bahia, Brazil

Organization: UNESCO Artists for Peace

What does he do? Gil challenged the Brazilian government in the 1960s by parading in the streets and playing his protest music. Because of this, he was jailed and later exiled. He moved to London, but returned to Brazil in 1972. In 2003, he became Brazil's Minister of Culture. He continues to be a political advocate today.

---

exiled: *banished from one's native land*

MEASHA BRUEGGERGOSMAN

Name: Measha Brueggergosman

Occupation: Classical singer

Born in: Fredericton, New Brunswick

Organizations: Canadian Goodwill Ambassador for Amref Health Africa, Learning Through the Arts, and World Wildlife Fund (WWF)

What does she do? Brueggergosman lends her voice and talents to children in areas affected by war in East Africa.

She says: "Being in Africa has been a humbling experience. Africa is not the destitute, hopeless continent that so many people think. [Africa is] the opposite, actually. It's a continent of energy, generosity, and hope. What is needed are the resources and training to put these [traits] into action. It's amazing to know that there are organizations like Amref ... to foster that hope."

destitute: *extremely poor; without basic necessities*

RUSSELL SIMMONS

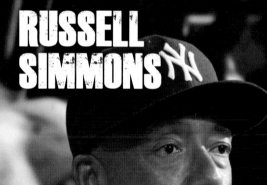

Name: Russell Simmons

Occupation: Music mogul, entrepreneur, founder of Def Jam, founder of Phat Farm

Born in: Queens, NY

Organizations: Co-Founder of the Rush Philanthropic Arts Foundation (Rush), Co-Chairman of the Hip-Hop Summit Action Network; supporter of People for the Ethical Treatment of Animals (PETA) and the Doe Fund

What does he do? Through Rush, Simmons, along with the other founders, is dedicated to providing inner New York City youth with exposure to the arts. The foundation is also dedicated to offering exhibitions to developing artists. Rush has two galleries, one in Brooklyn and one in Manhattan.

He says: "We believe that it is very important that kids get to practise using their creative mind as well as studying math and science. We built Rush Foundation to create awareness, but especially to promote opportunities for kids in inner city schools."

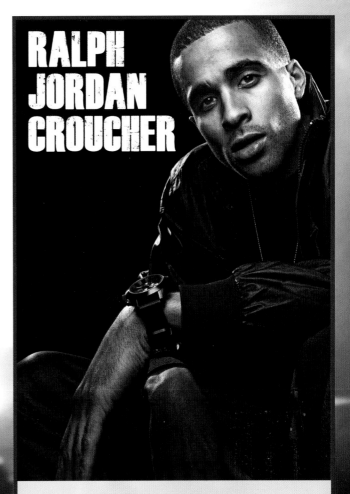

Name: Miriam Makeba

Occupation: Singer and civil rights activist

Born in: Johannesburg, South Africa

What did she do? Miriam Makeba, who died in 2008, was active in the fight against Apartheid in South Africa. After she spoke in front of the United Nations in 1963, she was exiled from South Africa. While in exile, she continued to record songs that brought awareness to the problems facing non-White South Africans. In 1999, Makeba was named Goodwill Ambassador for the Food and Agricultural Organization (FAO) of the United Nations. She worked alongside Graça Machel-Mandela, the wife of Nelson Mandela, on causes like child soldiers and HIV/AIDS.

She said: "Girls are the future mothers of our society, and it is important that we focus on their well-being."

Name: Ralph Jordan Croucher (a.k.a. JRDN)

Occupation: R&B singer

Born in: Halifax, Nova Scotia

What does he do? JRDN is currently a youth ambassador for Democracy 250 (D250). This initiative encourages Nova Scotia youth to be involved in their government. He also served as a delegate for the Citizen Voices program.

He says: "I am determined to make my mark. … To me that means giving back to my community, getting involved, and making a difference. …"

CONNECT IT

Go online and research another Black musician who gives back to his or her community. Write a short fact card about his or her work and share your fact card with a partner.

Index

Acknowledgements

Allen, Lillian. "Revolution from de Beat," from *Psychic Unrest* by Lillian Allen (1999) © Lillian Allen. Reprinted with permission of the author.

Backo, Njacko. "The Lost Toumkak." © Njacko Backo. Reprinted with permission of the author.

Photo Sources
Cover: singer–Umkehrer/Shutterstock.com; **4:** [girl–Samuel Borges Photography; piano design–Thomas Hartwig Laschon] Shutterstock.com; **6:** [pattern–anfisa focusova; texture–Jules_Kitano; djembe–taviphoto] Shutterstock.com; kora–iStockphoto.com/© GrigoriosMoraitis; **7:** mbira–Alex Weeks; [Kpanlogo–Anton_Ivanov; samba drummers–lazyllama] Shutterstock.com; **8:** Step Afrika–Leslie Frempong; alfaia drum–Lionel Baur; atabaque drum–CREATISTA/Shutterstock.com; **9:** [afro-cuban drums–Furtseff; cajón–Bildagentur Zoonar GmbH; steel pan drummers–Clive Chilvers] Shutterstock.com; **10:** [crowd–KR MEDIA Productions; green background–BR_WimStock; speaker–steveball] Shutterstock.com; Lilian Allen–Library and Archives Canada; **11:** drummer–MarkMcLaughlin; **12:** K'Naan–David Shankbone; Somalia–KerdaZz/Shutterstock.com; **14:** illustrations–Ho Che Anderson; **20:** Old Montreal–Benoit Brouillette; instruments–Katsiaryna Andronchyk/Shutterstock.com; **22:** Bob Marley–Eddie Mallin; background texture–Attitude/Shutterstock.com; **23:** The Skatalites–©ZUMAPRESS.com/Keystone Press; Leroy Sibbles–anviss; **24:** The Heptones–GAB Archive/Redferns/Getty Images; Judy Mowatt–Photo by Peter Mazel/Sunshine/KPA-ZUMA/KEYSTONE Press/KEYSTONE Press. (©) Copyright 2006 by Sunshine; **25:** Sugar Minott–Photo by David Corio/RedfernsGetty Images; Lee "Scratch" Perry–Photo by David Corio/Michael Ochs Archives/Getty Images; **26:** [hand with mic–apartment; swoosh–Daniel Abela; halftone pattern–almagami] Shutterstock.com; **27:** Dream Warriors–Graham Tucker/Redferns/Getty Images; Drake–John Steel/Shutterstock.com; Maestro Fresh Wes–Richard Lautens / GetStock.com; **28:** WondaGurl–Lucas Oleniuk / GetStock.com; Michie Mee–Tika Gregory; [record–donatas1205; microphone–Slavoljub Pantelic] Shutterstock.com; Mood Ruff–Jeremy Shields; k-os–danna (curious tangles); Reema Major–Isaiah Trickey/FilmMagic/Getty Images; **29:** televisions–trekandshoot/Shutterstock.com; Director X–Timothy M. Moore; **30:** [background–Hamara; speakers–Ensuper] Shutterstock.com; Portia White–Yousuf Karsh; **31:** Tony Young–Photo by Michael Stuparyk/Toronto Star via Getty Images; Keshia Chanté–Jayme Poisson / GetStock.com; **32:** Jully Black–TODD KOROL/Reuters /Landov; notepad–Kongsak/Shutterstock.com; **33:** woman–Jason Stitt/Shutterstock.com; Shad–©ZUMAPRESS.com/Keystone Press; **34:** Tiki Mercury Clarke–courtesy of Tiki Mercury-Clarke; [microphone–lem; notes–kentoh] Shutterstock.com; **36:** The Liyana Band–courtesy of Elinor Burkett; **37:** Bernie Pitters–Carlos Osorio / GetStock.com; **38:** Faith Nolan–courtesy of Anne deHaas; [background–Nagib; sheet music–Kate Swansh] Shutterstock.com; **40:** Kellylee Evans–Clive Chilvers/Getstock.com; music notes–Ramona Kaulitzki/Shutterstock.com; **41:** DJ L'Oqenz–John Shearer / Staff / Getty Images; Eb Reinbergs–courtesy of Eb Reinbergs; **42:** Karen Burke–York University/Karen Burke; Del F. Cowie–courtesy of Del F. Cowie; **43:** Jimi Hendrix–Arup Malakar; [lights–ilolab; band–Francesco Abrignani; crowd–melis] Shutterstock.com; **44:** crowd–Annette Shaff/Shutterstock.com; Jully Black–Damien D.; **45:** [Alicia Keys–Everett Collection; Kardinal Offishall–Stacey Newman] Shutterstock.com; Gilberto Gil–Thesupermat; **46:** Measha Brueggergosman–Damien D; Russell Simmons–Brett Weinstein; **47:** Miriam Makeba–cdrin/Shutterstock.com; Ralph Jordan Croucher–Maplecore.